MW00618127

Here's what people are saying about *The Step Dynamic*™

"The Step Dynamic gives sound advice on how to grow your business and underlines the importance of balance in the whole process. I recommend it."

—Ken Blanchard, coauthor
The One Minute Manager and The Secret

"The Step Dynamic's relationship between capabilities and sales growth is one of the most powerful concepts a business owner should understand."

—Noreen King, president, Evolve
Manufacturing Technologies, Inc.,
one of *Inc.* magazine's 2005
"Inc. 500" fastest-growing companies

"The Step Dynamic provides growing businesses with several important lessons in a fun to read format. It clearly illustrates the danger in letting sales outpace capacity or capacity outpace sales. *The Step Dynamic* is an interesting read that is time well spent for an entrepreneur at any level of growth."

—Winslow "Bud" Johnson,
author *Powerhouse Marketing Plans*

"Informative and thoroughly entertaining. The authors have integrated a powerful concept with an interesting story line. Bravo!"

—Kraig W. Kramers, business speaker,
author, consultant, and former CEO
of eight different businesses

"Having sold over eight hundred businesses over the last twenty-four years, I have talked to thousands of business owners. Many of these entrepreneurs struggled with the issues set forth in the text, and their businesses would have been more valuable had the owners been able to solve those problems. The book is a fast read, but provides valuable insight for time challenged entrepreneurs."

—Ronald V. Chernak, president, First Business Brokers, Ltd.; former chairman of the International Business Brokers Association

The Step Dynamic is required reading for those wanting to grow their business. These simple, yet precise business principles can help the smart business owner avoid common pitfalls and to grow effectively and efficiently. No matter what industry you're in, you will relate to the concepts and solutions provided within."

—Dirk R. Hobbs,owner, *Medical Voyce, Inc.* publisher, *M.D. News Magazines*, Colorado

The Step Dynamic™

A Powerful Strategy
for Successfully Growing
Your Business

by Laddie Blaskowski
and Judy Blaskowski

GroCorp Publications
Colorado Springs, Colorado

The Step Dynamic: A Powerful Strategy for Successfully Growing Your Business

The advice and strategies contained herein may not be suitable for your situation. You should consult with a professional where appropriate. Neither the publisher nor the authors shall be liable for any loss of profit or any other commercial damages, including but not limited to special, incidental, consequential, or other damages. Characters and companies mentioned in this book are purely fictitious and any similarities to people and/or organizations are unintentional.

Visit the authors' website at www.BusinessTruths.com for resources on business growth or to subscribe to the free monthly newsletter, *BusinessTruths® Monthly.*

ISBN 13: 978-1-933981-35-2
ISBN: 1-933981-35-0

Library of Congress Control Number: 2006926287

Printed in the United States of America

Cover and internal graphics by Thomason Design Center, Inc., Colorado Springs, CO

ATTENTION CORPORATIONS, UNIVERSITIES, PROFESSIONAL ASSOCIATIONS: Quantity discounts are available on bulk purchases of this book for reselling, educational purposes, subscription incentives, gifts, or fund-raising. Customized books can be created to feature your organization. For information, contact our Special Sales Department at 719-232-0710.

To Bruce Beebe, our mentor and friend.

Table of Contents

Creating the Business of Your Dreams

If you're like most entrepreneurs, you dream of seeing your business grow.

When you started your company, you expected it to provide a flexible lifestyle, financial security and challenges you would enjoy. You were supposed to control the business, seeing the fruits of your labor come about through consistent and manageable growth.

Regrettably, for many entrepreneurs this dream is just that—a dream.

As a banker, business consultant and speaker, I have had the pleasure of meeting thousands of business owners throughout my career. Instead of describing a smooth growth process in their companies, many have told a different story.

As their companies grew, the owners found day-to-day operations were a constant struggle. Instead of controlling their businesses, all too often their businesses seemingly took over their lives. They tried to make the right decisions but new problems always kept cropping up. Growth brought cash flow troubles, employee issues, sales concerns and management problems.

Growing a business doesn't have to be that way!

If you understand how businesses grow...if you recognize how your current stage of growth is affecting your company and take the right steps...then you can achieve your dream.

The Step Dynamic is a revolutionary new business tool that can help! This book will explore The Step Dynamic principles, why they're important and how they can bring back the joy of owning your business. Take a journey with our fictional characters as they explore The Step Dynamic and learn to view your own business in a new and different way.

May your business grow and prosper, and may you achieve your personal dreams!

—*Laddie Blaskowski*

Chapter One

Feeling the Pain of Business Growth

John Clairren reached for the alarm at 4:45, hit the snooze button and groaned as he pulled the covers over his head. He desperately needed more sleep but now that he was semi-awake, he was afraid he wouldn't be able to drift off again. His mind was suddenly filled with the same jumble of aggravation and swirling thoughts that had prevented him from going to sleep until after midnight.

After a few minutes of deep breathing in an unsuccessful attempt to go back to the pleasant dream he'd been having, he gave up, shut off the alarm and crept quietly out of bed to avoid waking his wife, Karen. Truth be told, he actually felt like giving her a little shove so she could have a taste of getting up as early as he did. But he knew that wouldn't do much for what little awake-time they had together anymore, so he resisted the temptation.

He padded across the carpet to the bathroom, turned on the shower, then stopped and stared at himself in the mirror. He looked like what he was: a tired, dumpy, middle-aged guy. Turning sideways, he inhaled deeply, threw out his chest and sucked in his stomach in an effort to bring back the illusion of his former physique. But the effort was too much for him. He blew the air out of his lungs and watched his pectoral muscles seem to melt away and ooze into his waistline. "John, you look like roadkill!" he told himself.

As he climbed into the shower, he started thinking about the day ahead and some of the work waiting on his desk. He realized that once again he was actually dreading going to work and wishing he had some other type of job. "What kind of moron was I to think it would be easy and pleasant to run my own business?" he asked himself for the hundredth time.

John hadn't always felt that way about being a business owner, but lately he'd been having these kinds of negative thoughts more frequently. He was a fairly average 40-year-old guy, except all of his adult life he'd had the entrepreneurial "bug"—the inner voice that nags at a person and says, "Why not?"

And so, nine years earlier, he had left a lucrative position with a large corporation to launch Clairren Security, which manufactured security system components. He was now respected in the community as a successful business owner. He drove a nice car, lived in a spacious house in an upscale community, had a wonderful family, and other people thought he had an enviable lifestyle as a self-made entrepreneur. But John had an ugly little secret. People thought John ran his own business. In reality, John's business ran him.

In the first few years, as is the case with most start-ups, the company had struggled. But then the product line had taken off and the business had started growing. John had been excited by the huge increases in sales and the prospect of seeing his dreams realized. He felt like a real hotshot and thought he had surely hit the big time.

His enthusiasm soon diminished, however, because as the business grew, so did the problems. Day-to-day operations became increasingly frustrating, and it seemed he was constantly putting out fires and worrying about cash flow. Employee issues cropped up, his decisions weren't always the best, and it was hard to figure out where to focus his time and efforts. On a personal level, the long hours he was forced to put in taxed his family life. He never had adequate time to devote to his wife or attend his kids' activities.

John was realizing the business he had started as a way to gain freedom, create wealth, have time to indulge his passion for fly fishing and improve his family's lifestyle had become exactly the opposite. Instead, it had turned into a time and energy-gobbling beast that was wearing him out and eroding his confidence.

He had begun to feel like a fish caught in a net—trapped by frustrations he couldn't seem to escape.

Today John was having a rare opportunity to sneak away for lunch with a friend. He had known Dave Johnson for a number of years and had a great deal of respect for him, both on a personal level and as a businessman.

As they sat down to lunch, Dave asked John how his business was going.

"Oh, fine," John answered.

"In my experience, 'fine' doesn't usually mean everything's okay. So what's it really like?"

John stared hard out the restaurant window for a minute and then turned to his friend. "You know, I'm so tired and frustrated that there are days when I simply want to call it quits." Seeing Dave's raised eyebrows, he decided to take it a step further. "In fact, some days I actually wish I had a *real* job. You know— go to work, come home, leave work at the office, enjoy being at home and actually see my wife and kids from time to time. Collect a nice paycheck every couple of weeks...."

Dave covered his face with his hands in a gesture of mock horror. "Oh, no, John, not a *real* job. Tell me it hasn't come to this!" He chuckled softly and said, "Man, I hate to hear you're having such a struggle. I had no idea. The last time we got together you sounded completely positive and had just gotten a bunch of new sales. So what's brought on all this negativity?"

John sighed and scratched his head. "Well, this may sound crazy, but I think those new sales are actually creating a bunch of new problems. In fact, the more sales we've gotten and the more we've grown, the worse it's gotten. The headaches have increased exponentially with the growth. I often wonder if it's all worth it."

"Oh boy, that brings back memories. I know exactly what you mean," nodded Dave. "I've been there."

John looked up in surprise. "You're kidding me, right? Whenever we talk, you always seem to be doing just great and business always sounds good. When were you ever in my situation?"

"You just didn't know me ten years ago. My life was very similar to what you're describing. I wasn't happy about it but didn't know how to fix things."

"Well, it's obvious you *did* fix things because you seem to be in pretty good shape now. So what did you do differently?"

"I learned about something called The Step Dynamic."

John was intrigued "What's The Step Dynamic? Some kind of exercise program?"

Dave took a sip of his soda. "No, The Step Dynamic is a way of looking at your business that helps you understand how it grows and what you need to do as it grows. Basically, how to make the right decisions at the right time. I learned all about it from a man named Bruce Baxleigh."

"And what makes this Bruce guy such an expert?"

"Well, he's a highly successful entrepreneur, although he's retired now. He's owned three different companies over his lifetime. The guy is sharp and really understands what makes a business tick."

"How did you hook up with him?"

"I met Bruce while he was still working at the last company he owned. We got to know each other and I told him about some of the problems I was experiencing. He explained to me why my company was struggling and what I needed to do to change it, so I followed his advice."

"That's it?"

"That's it, my friend. Now business is good and I'm enjoying owning it again. I make more money and the place is easier to run. I understand what I need to be doing and when I need to do it, as the company grows. The Step Dynamic taught me to understand where my time and energy needed to be focused for my business to thrive."

"Really?" John scratched his head. "So tell me how this Step Dynamic thing works."

"No can do. Bruce has to do it."

"What do you mean Bruce has to do it?

Why can't you explain it to me?"

"Because that's how it works. You'll have to meet Bruce yourself, but I'd be happy to arrange a meeting for you."

"So why would this guy be willing to take his time to meet with me? He doesn't even know me."

"But I know you! Trust me, if I ask him to meet with you he'll be glad to do it. I don't want to waste his time, though, so if I set up a lunch meeting will you commit to it?"

John stared at his friend and thought about it. He had known and respected Dave for years. Dave ran a successful company and had a nice life. Dave got to go fishing on weekends. John hadn't had time to go fishing for ages.

"Just because I meet this Bruce Baxleigh doesn't mean I have to sign up for anything, does it?"

"Of course not. You two might not even hit it off but I think you'd find it beneficial to meet with him. Why don't you just try it? What have you got to lose besides buying his lunch?"

John thought for a few minutes. *What do I have to lose?* "Okay, go ahead and set it up. Just let me know when and where, and I'll be there."

"Great! I'll call you. Now, let me tell you about the seven-pound trout I caught last weekend!"

Chapter Two

What Is This Step Dynamic Anyway?

On the appointed day, John walked uncertainly into the restaurant, told the hostess he was meeting someone named Bruce, and was escorted to a high-walled booth tucked into a far back corner of the restaurant. *Good, no one can hear our conversation,* he thought.

Seated at the table was a man about 65 years old or so. Balding and white haired, the man had a handsome, friendly face. He looked up and flashed John a warm smile. "You must be John. I'm Bruce Baxleigh."

He slid out of the booth to stand and offer John his hand. Bruce was not a particularly tall man, but appeared quite fit and his handshake felt like steel. While his eyes were direct and strong, the deep laugh lines in the corners gave evidence of a good sense of humor. His resonant voice was pleasant and made John feel at ease.

"Yes, I'm John Clairren. It's nice to meet you, Bruce."

"I'm glad to meet you too, John. Dave told me a little about your conversation last week and thought I might be able to help you."

He's certainly direct, John thought as they eased themselves into their seats at the booth.

"I have to admit, I'm a bit vague about exactly what you do but Dave was extremely enthusiastic about how you helped him."

Bruce smiled and looked straight into John's eyes as if trying to ascertain more about his character. "Well, John, I'd like to teach you what I've learned about the process involved in growing a business, which is something I call The Step Dynamic. I think it can help solve a lot of the issues Dave said you're dealing with right now and can help your business be far more successful."

John immediately liked his straightforwardness and sensed he was a person of integrity. He felt Bruce was genuinely interested in helping him.

The server interrupted their conversation when she arrived with menus and proceeded to take their drink orders. They took a few minutes to scan the menus and gave their orders when she returned with their drinks.

"That all sounds great but it also sounds too good to be true," John admitted. "Although, I've got to say, it would be a lifesaver for me if I could get myself and my company out of the situation we're currently experiencing." John paused to collect his thoughts as he looked around the restaurant, and shook his head. "I'm tired, Bruce, just very, very tired. I thought owning a business was supposed to be more fun and give my life flexibility. But running my company isn't fun anymore. It's started to feel like a burden rather than a blessing. Does that make any sense to you?"

"You're right; it is supposed to be fun," Bruce responded. "Businesses aren't supposed to be all-consuming and take over your life. I firmly believe business ownership should be a pleasant, rewarding experience. Now, I'm not saying you should have unrealistic expectations, because all companies experience problems from time to time. But I believe a business can and should operate smoothly most of the time and the owner should enjoy owning it."

"I'd sure love for my company to run that way," John admitted.

"I'd like to help you, John, if you'll allow me to do so. However, I realize that aside from Dave's recommendation, you really don't know me from Adam. You're probably wondering what's in it for me." John nodded in agreement, so Bruce continued. "How about if I tell you my own story and you can decide if I'm someone you'd like to work with?"

"Fair enough."

"When I got out of college with my MBA, I thought I was a big deal and far too smart to have to work for someone else. I wanted to be my own boss and thought I was surely destined to be the superhero of the business world. So I started a small manufacturing operation with every expectation of striking it rich.

"Unfortunately, I had a lot of book knowledge but not a lick of common sense. I made some unbelievably colossal mistakes—extremely poor decisions—and in less than two years, the business went down the tubes."

John grimaced. "Ouch! That had to hurt!"

"You bet it hurt. I think my pride was hurt more than anything but the old pocketbook didn't feel so great either. For a while, I found it necessary to have a real job so I could support my wife and pay off the business debt. But I wasn't happy working for someone else."

"Then we have something in common. Not wanting to work for someone else, I mean."

Bruce smiled. "I really wanted to be in business for myself so once I was back on my feet, I got a loan and bought another small company. This time it was reasonably successful in the sense that it was profitable but it was a struggle. It seemed as though I'd take one step forward and two steps backward. I could see the next level on the horizon but could never figure out how to get there. And, man, was I working hard!"

"Ah, something else we have in common!" interjected John.

Bruce grinned. "I knew I was exhausted and grumpy, but I didn't realize how unpleasant I had become until I came home one evening and discovered my wife had placed a box of PMS medicine on my dinner plate!" Both men burst out laughing.

"That's hilarious!" John exclaimed. "But the grumpiness and exhaustion sure sound familiar!"

"I thought you might understand," Bruce said, nodding in agreement. "Anyway, I decided getting along with my wife was more important than being in business for myself, so I sold the business for exactly what I had paid for it. That wasn't bad, except I was forced to take another *real* job in order to support my family, especially since we had a toddler at home."

The waitress arrived with their food, so the conversation paused while she laid the plates on the table. "Now we come to business number three. I had a terrific idea, was able to obtain financing and started another manufacturing company. However, this time I sat down beforehand and analyzed exactly what had gone wrong in the first two companies I'd owned.

"I met with other business owners to brainstorm ideas and a pattern began to emerge. That's how I developed The Step Dynamic theory. As a result, running the third company was vastly easier because I finally understood how to successfully grow a business and take it to the next level. I knew the secret of making the right decisions at the right time. Over a period of ten years, I took my company from zero to many millions in value. We eventually went public and I served as CEO until a few years ago when I retired."

John's eyes grew large and he whistled softly. "Wow!" was all he could think of to say.

"I'm financially set for life and feel it's my 'calling,' so to speak, to share my knowledge with business owners who are struggling with some of the same issues I've faced. I feel blessed and want to give back."

Again, all John could think of to say was, "Wow."

"I have a lot of information to share with you, but here's the most important thing you need to remember as your company grows: capabilities and sales do not increase in a linear manner."

"What do you mean?" asked John.

"I used to think business growth went something like this. You'd start out with some capabilities and obtain some sales. You'd add some more capabilities and grow a little more, with your sales and capabilities increasing at approximately the same pace. Sort of like inching your way up a ramp. That's what I mean by a linear process.

"Because of viewing business that way, I was always in trouble, always fighting fires and didn't have the right employees in the right places. I was making what I thought were good decisions but I was making them at the wrong time. Growth brought a whole lot of problems and frustrations."

John looked confused. "I'm not sure I'm getting this. If that's not how companies grow, then how do they grow?"

"It's a concept that's easy to understand once you can visualize it. Think about a ramp and a staircase. Rather than growing in a linear manner, as if you were walking up the ramp, businesses grow in steps as if you were climbing the staircase.

"Now let's define what I mean by capabilities. Capabilities are all of the resources in your company that allow it to operate."

"You mean things like equipment, computers and office space?" John asked.

"Those things are certainly important parts of your capabilities," Bruce answered. "But it takes a lot more than those components to make your business capable of operating. Capabilities include the employees you have in place and how you train them. They include the systems and controls you've developed, and your ability to market and sell your products. Your company's technology, operations management and customer service are all parts of your capabilities, as is one of the most crucial parts of your capabilities—your ability to finance the business."

"That makes sense," John said.

"When you start your business, you must have a certain level of capabilities to make even one dollar in sales and those capabilities can carry you to a certain level. For example, you're a manufacturer, John, so you had to start your business with certain equipment, employees, space, inventory, systems and controls. You needed those things whether you intended to make just one dollar or a million dollars in sales. Correct?"

"That's right," replied John.

"Let me draw you a picture of what happens next." Bruce reached for a yellow legal pad sitting on the table and drew a graph.

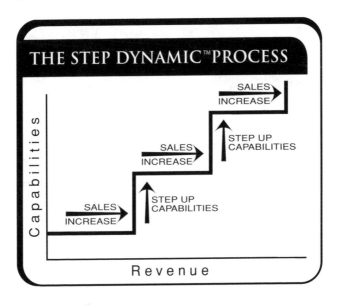

"I call this The Step Dynamic Process. If you continue to increase sales, you'll reach a point in your business where your capabilities are no longer adequate for your sales volume

27

and you'll have to step up your capabilities. Let's say that point would be sales of a million dollars. You may need more capital, additional employees, another layer of management, more space, increased systems and controls, and so on.

"But here's the critical concept: these increases in necessary capabilities won't happen gradually. They will most likely happen all at the same time. That's where the problems arise."

"I never thought about it in that way," admitted John.

"An interesting concept, isn't it?" Bruce continued, "Let's say with your new capabilities you can now handle up to $3 million in sales. You're doing just over $1 million in sales but all of the new equipment, bigger space and the additional employees are costing you a bundle. So you've got to add more sales or the overhead will kill you."

John thought for a moment. "I suppose if you were to increase your sales beyond $3 million, your capabilities would become inadequate again."

"Exactly!" exclaimed Bruce. "Now you would have to make another step up. In my case, the first business I owned never even made it off the ground. The second company was viable and I wanted it to grow, but I could never seem to take it to the next level. I got stuck in one place because I couldn't get the connection right between my sales and capabilities."

"My company's sales keep climbing, which I had thought would be a good thing, but sometimes I feel absolutely buried," John said.

Bruce nodded. "Once you understand your business will grow in steps, you've got to understand how to handle those steps. Certain things need to be done at each phase along the steps. If you don't do those things, you waste time and money. Running the company becomes extremely frustrating and, in a worst-case scenario, the company could even tank.

"Now let's look at what I call The Step Dynamic diagram." Bruce quickly sketched another graph.

"As you can see, I've written A, B, Y and Z on the diagram to represent the four critical places where a business can be along the steps. The A and B represent normal stages in business. The Y and Z represent problematic situations."

"What exactly are those four critical places? How do they work?" asked John. He

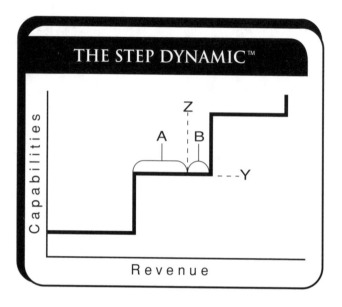

was hooked now and wanted to know more. "I'd like to understand how this affects my business — where my business is on the graph and how I should move forward."

"Ah, that's where we commit to working together. I'll be happy to teach you about how The Step Dynamic works and how to successfully handle the growth steps, but I will need a commitment from you."

"What kind of commitment?"

"You need to commit two full, consecutive weekdays to working with me."

"Two full days?" John scratched his head. "Boy, I don't know, Bruce. Is that much time really necessary? With everything going on, it's going to be tough to get away for two full days."

"John, that's precisely the point. You're here talking to me today because it is so hard for you to get away. It's not only necessary; it's required. It takes time to conduct our field trips and I require a commitment so none of us wastes our time."

"Field trips? What kind of field trips?"

"I'm not going to merely explain The Step Dynamic to you. I believe it's a better learning experience if you can actually see it in action, so we're going to visit four companies that have been at the four critical areas on the steps."

John was skeptical. "Are you telling me those business owners are going to be willing to open up to a total stranger about how they run their companies?"

"That's exactly what I mean. I can guarantee you'll learn more from those entrepreneurs than you would ever learn from just hearing me talk. So, what'll it be?"

John scribbled a few things on his notepad and looked up at Bruce. "I can do this. My company can survive two days without my being in the building and if any fires come up, I'll deal with them after you and I are finished each day. It's clear I need some help because I haven't been able to do this on my own. But hold on a minute. Before we plan any of this, I need to know what it's going to cost me."

"Can't tell you that, John."

"I beg your pardon?"

"I said, I can't tell you. You're just going to have to trust me. I promise the fee will be fair and easily affordable. If you are in any way dissatisfied with our time together, you don't have to pay me anything at all."

John was shocked and his face showed it. "Well, I can't ask for anything more fair than that."

"I'd like to get on this right away so I'll go ahead and set up our appointments. How about this Thursday and Friday?"

"I guess that's as good a time as any. I'll get things squared away at the office."

"Terrific! Unless you hear otherwise from me, I'll pick you up at your office at 9:00 on Thursday morning." Bruce stood and stretched his back. "Thanks for having lunch with me, John. This has been great. I'll see you on Thursday, then." He reached to shake John's hand, snatched up the check with a sly grin and strode toward the cash register.

John sat back in his chair, feeling both overwhelmed and amazed by Bruce and his exuberance. He couldn't believe he had just committed to taking two whole days away from his business. *Okay,* he said to himself. *What have you done?* He laughed softly to himself as he made his way to the front of the restaurant and realized he was actually looking forward to this adventure. *Field trips!*

Chapter Three

Shooting Past the Step—Too Much of a Good Thing Can Kill You!

At 9:00 on Thursday morning, John's cell phone rang as he sat at his desk. It was Bruce, calling to say he was waiting in the parking lot. John picked up a sheet of instructions he had scribbled, grabbed his briefcase and travel coffee mug, and walked over to the receptionist's desk to leave the instructions for her. He opened the door to the shop and peered in to make sure all was well, then walked out of the building.

Bruce was waiting for him in a black luxury sedan. "Good morning!" his voice pealed cheerfully as John opened the door. "Are you raring to go?"

"Yes, I am. So where are we heading first?"

"We're going to see my good friend, Bob Pryce. You'll like him—he's a very outgoing guy."

They drove across town to an industrial area and pulled into the parking lot of a long, low cinderblock building. One section bore a large sign reading "Pryce Concrete." Bruce drove to a parking space directly in front of what appeared to be an office area and stopped the car.

"I know this company," remarked John. "They did quite a bit of work at my neighbor's house last summer and did a very nice job. I was thinking of having them give me an estimate for re-pouring my driveway."

"I had them do some work at my own house last summer," replied Bruce. "I've known Bob for a couple of years now."

They went into the tidy but sparsely furnished front office, and Bruce spoke to the receptionist. She immediately got up and walked down a short hall to an office doorway, then returned to say Bob would be with them in just a minute. A few seconds later, a large, barrel-chested man, who appeared to be in his early fifties, came out and walked toward them with a broad grin on his face.

"Bruce, great to see you!" he exclaimed in a booming voice as he thrust out his hand.

"Great to see you too, Bob. I'd like to introduce John Clairren, the man I told you about on the phone."

Bob turned his attention to John and gave him an equally gregarious welcome, pumping his hand enthusiastically and slapping him on the back. "I'm glad you could come. I like showing off my little Slab of Heaven. Get it? Slab of Heaven? We're a concrete company."

What a character! John thought as he returned the handshake. "Yes, I know. You're a darned good concrete company too. I've seen one of your jobs at my neighbor's house and you guys do excellent work."

Bob beamed like a kid with a big, red A-plus on a test paper. "That's good to hear. We always appreciate positive feedback on our jobs. Well, then, let's get down to business!" He had a deep, powerful voice and it occurred to John that between his voice and his size, Bob could seem formidable to a lazy employee or a badly behaved teenager. Good thing the guy had a sense of humor!

As Bob led the others down the hall, he remarked, "Bruce tells me you're a fisherman, John."

John looked quizzically at Bruce, who shrugged his shoulders.

"Well, yes, I do love to fish whenever I can," John admitted.

"So do I! In fact, I was ice fishing a while back with my brother-in-law, Herman. Man, Herman was pulling them in one right after the other! I couldn't figure out why he was catching so many fish when I hadn't even gotten a nibble. So I asked him what his secret was. You know what he said?"

"No, what?"

Bob stopped in the hallway and turned to face the other two men. With a completely serious look on his face, he said "Mu mat to meep da merms marm."

Bruce smiled knowingly and John looked confused.

Bob continued, "So I said, 'What?' and Herman said it again! 'Mu mat to meep da merms marm.'

"I said, 'Herman, I can't understand a darned thing you're saying.' So he spit into his hand and said, 'You've got to keep the worms warm!'"

Bob burst out laughing, his massive torso shaking with mirth. John and Bruce couldn't help but laugh, more from Bob's reaction than the joke itself. Bob shook his head to clear it, took a handkerchief from his pocket and dabbed at his eyes. "Okay, I guess now we really do need to get down to business."

He led the other two men down the narrow hallway, through some double doors and into a shop. They toured the shop and then went through more doors into an outdoor work area, where a cement truck was just getting ready to leave for a job. John had never visited a cement company before, so he had a number of questions that Bob readily answered.

After they finished touring the work areas, Bob led them into a small conference room furnished with a long, metal-topped table and a sizeable white board attached to one wall. A smaller table was pushed up against another wall and held a coffee maker and mugs.

Bob poured three cups of steaming black coffee, which he set on the conference table, along with creamer and sugar canisters. Then he took a seat and looked from Bruce to John expectantly.

"Bob, why don't you start?" Bruce prompted.

"Okay. Bruce asked me to do most of the talking today, so I'll get right to the point by telling you my story."

He paused and waited for John to finish extracting a yellow legal pad and pen from his leather case. As John started taking notes, Bob continued, "I met Bruce about two years ago, at a time when I was facing a crisis with this business. Now, I don't have a lot of formal business education but I've got a lot of common sense. I'm pretty street-smart and I know the concrete business inside and out. I had always run this company pretty darned well, but two years ago I found myself in a jam and couldn't figure out how to get out of it."

"What kind of jam?" John asked. Then, taking a chance at a little humor of his own, he ventured, "I suppose you're going to say you were stuck in cement."

Bob blinked hard in surprise, looked over at Bruce, and then let out a hearty laugh. "Oh, that's a good one! Stuck in cement!"

Bruce just shook his head and smiled.

"I like this guy!" Bob said. "Okay, seriously, I had started out with nothing and had grown this business to about a $5 million level. Things were running smoothly and I was as happy as a tick on a hound dog. It was fun and I thought owning this company had to be the most rewarding thing in the world.

"But then things changed. On the surface, it seemed positive. The whole construction industry started taking off and so did my sales. In a very short period of time, my revenue jumped to around $6.5 million."

"That sounds pretty good," said John as he smiled. "Most people wouldn't mind having a $1.5 million jump in business!"

"Yeah, that's probably what most people would think. But it wasn't so simple. I had been forced to hire more employees and had brought on a couple more estimators. I had thought this big influx in sales was a great thing but it got to the point where every day seemed like a major hassle. I wasn't enjoying my work anymore.

"I was making mistakes right and left. I needed to buy a bunch of new stuff but was having trouble financing it. I went from working about 50 hours a week to working 80 or 90 hours a week. I was dog-tired and feeling pretty miserable a lot of the time."

John felt he should speak up. "A lot of what you're describing in the way of problems sounds very similar to what I've been going through."

"It's pretty bad when you don't enjoy your own business any more!" exclaimed Bob. "This brings us to about two years ago, which is when I met Bruce through my brother-in-law. Bruce sat down with me and I explained what had been going on. He drew me a picture that clearly showed what had happened in my business."

Bob turned to Bruce and asked, "Do you want to draw it or should I?"

Bruce leaned back in his chair, crossed his legs, and said, "You go ahead, Bob. You know it well."

Bob stood, walked to the white board and drew a diagram.

"Bruce said he's already told you about The Step Dynamic concept. This little number is a picture of what he calls 'Shooting Past the Step.' Do you see the $5 million position on the graph? That's the level where my company's capabilities were when I started receiving the new sales. But see how the Y is clear out to the right and off the staircase? At that point we were bringing in about $6.5 million in sales.

The sales had increased way past the capabilities my company had to handle them, and we were in trouble. We simply didn't have the infrastructure in this company for that kind of sales volume. Five million in sales, yes. Six and a half million in sales, no way.

"Despite the higher sales, my margins were going down because of mistakes and problems. Good old Bruce helped me see I had four choices." Bob paused in his narrative to write a list below the diagram on the whiteboard:

1. Stay put.
2. Step up.
3. Step back and regroup.
4. Sell.

Turning from the whiteboard, he continued. "First, I could stay where I was, continue to struggle along and see if the business could survive. Well, that didn't sound good to me because that was the current situation and was the reason I'd called on Bruce in the first place. Besides, at the rate I was going

I figured I'd probably drop dead from exhaustion in the process.

"The second choice was to immediately step up by adding capabilities. Bruce and I discussed this option at length and I realized it would be a big mistake."

John was surprised. "I don't understand. Why would it be a mistake to increase your capabilities to match your sales volume?"

"I think Bruce should jump in here," suggested Bob.

Bruce began, "Keep in mind, John, that it wasn't simply a matter of Bob buying another truck or piece of equipment. To keep up with the huge increase in sales volume, he needed to add significant capabilities in a very short period of time. Remember our definition of capabilities: all of the resources in your company that allow it to operate. He needed improved systems and controls, additional financing, key people in key positions and so on.

"Put yourself in Bob's shoes for a moment. You're already tired, frustrated, working impossibly long hours, and making mistakes right and left. In order for you to quickly increase your capabilities, you're going to have to go all out with some big decisions and take major action."

John nodded his head thoughtfully. "Yeah, I can see that."

"Obtaining additional financing from your bank to cover the costs of increasing your capabilities has to be a priority and can be a time consuming undertaking. At the same point, you're going to have to build in some additional systems and controls to make sure things don't fall through the cracks. You'll need more employees, which requires interviewing, hiring and training. There will be even more fires to put out and you'll have customer service issues that come with running a higher volume company.

"You see, it takes a great deal of time and effort to add a significant amount of capabilities. When you're in crisis mode, as Bob was, dealing with those things on top of what you're already doing is very tough. And if you were to continue adding sales at this point, it would create a bigger monster."

"Whew! I see what you mean," admitted John. "You could be doubling your workload. You'd burn out in no time!"

Bruce continued "Yes, and you could also end up failing completely. When you get this bogged down in trying to simply run your business, things fall through the cracks and customer service usually suffers. Your customers get fed up and leave. I've observed that people who increase their capabilities too quickly because their sales have shot off the step usually end up throwing a lot of money at their companies. But it's seldom successful and they end up going backwards anyway. Bob, why don't you continue with your story?"

Bob obliged. "So stepping up didn't sound at all like a good idea. The third thing I could do was back up and regroup, and I didn't like that idea either. It would mean having to tell customers we couldn't do their work. We'd probably lose a bunch of them—maybe some of the customers I'd worked for years to keep. And I'd probably have to lay off some people. The idea of going backwards didn't appeal to me at all!

"The fourth choice was to sell the business, which was the worst choice out of the bunch in my book. The company's situation was driving me crazy, but it was still *my* company and I had worked hard to build it. I wasn't ready to chuck it all in."

"Man," muttered John, shaking his head. "Those all sound pretty drastic to me, but I can't think of any other possible solutions to the problem. So what did you do?"

"Well, I did a lot of analysis and soul searching, and finally decided the best course to take was backing up to a comfortable revenue level—about $5 million dollars—and regroup. It wasn't an easy thing to do. I had to tell my salesperson to back off and not sell so hard any more. I was forced to let one of my estimators go and good estimators are not easy to find.

"The employee situation was bad but the customer issue was worse. If I turned them away because I didn't have the time or capabilities to do their jobs, I could lose them forever. And I had worked hard to get them in the first place. I was in a position where I couldn't keep some customers even if they wanted to hire us."

"What a terrible situation!" John interjected.

"I thought so. I didn't want to lose customers forever. So instead of calling anyone and canceling orders, I simply filled the existing orders, raised prices on new ones, and some customers left on their own. It was tough, but I didn't 'fire' them so there was no animosity and some have even returned since then.

"I still want to grow the company and I will eventually. Actually, I expect the step-up to take place around the first of the year. But this time I'm preparing for it and I'm going to do it the right way. In the meantime, we're doing well and I'm enjoying running the company again."

"That's terrific!" John exclaimed. "You obviously learned a lot of valuable things from the whole experience, didn't you?"

"Oh, I definitely learned a lot, that's for sure. But it was a very hard lesson to learn. Allowing my sales to shoot past my capabilities was one of the worst mistakes I ever made. I just wish I'd learned it all sooner. I could have saved myself a lot of worry, time and money, and would probably have a bigger and better business today."

John thought for a moment. "I have one last question for you guys," he said. "Is it always necessary to grow a business? I mean, if you're operating at a comfortable level, is there any reason why you couldn't just stay where you are and not have to worry about growth at all?"

"It all depends, John," Bruce answered. "If you're in a business that doesn't have a lot of competition or your industry doesn't change very much, you're probably safe to stay where you are. However, if you've got a lot of competitors or you're in a fast changing industry, you can't afford to sit still or your competition will roll right over you."

"Yeah, like a cement truck!" Bob added as he chuckled.

"Oh, no, more concrete humor!" Bruce said, smiling. He brought the meeting to a close by thanking Bob for taking time out of his day to meet with them. As they said their goodbyes, Bob gave John a parting bit of advice. "Learn this Step Dynamic stuff. Bruce is a good guy and he won't steer you wrong!"

As Bruce and John headed off to lunch, they discussed Bob's experience.

"Bob learned his Step Dynamic lessons the hard way," commented Bruce. "Letting your sales grow way beyond your capabilities has about the same effect as if you're landing an airplane and overshoot the runway. You usually crash and burn." He turned into the restaurant. "This afternoon I'm going to introduce you to a company that had problems even worse than Bob's."

John had enjoyed his morning and had learned a lot, so he looked forward to the afternoon session. It had been refreshing to hear someone else talk so candidly about business problems and solutions. This was an entirely new experience for him.

"I can't wait to see what's next, Bruce!"

Chapter Four

Stepping Up Too Soon—What If You Build a Business and No One Comes?

After lunch, the two men once again climbed into Bruce's car. John was eager to see what he'd learn at this afternoon's session. He was still digesting what he'd learned that morning from Bob and suspected the afternoon would be just as interesting.

As Bruce started the car he was enthusiastic. "Are you ready to absorb some more great information?"

"You bet. I'm learning you're a never-ending source of information."

"I'm very glad you feel that way!"

This time they drove to a light industrial area in a different section of town. When the car pulled into the parking lot of Boorley Medical, John was immediately impressed by the modern looking facility. It was a large, two-story building, covered completely on the front side with reflective windows. A small area of ornate landscaping flowed away from either side of the front door.

Once inside the building, the reception area was equally sleek and sophisticated. It had obviously been professionally decorated and contained modern looking chrome and leather furniture, an assortment of interesting lamps and pictures, and a number of tropical plants. The walls were painted a flat gray color, with the exception of the wall behind the reception desk, which was covered in a richly textured maroon wallpaper. Backlit silver letters spelling Boorley Medical stood out several inches from the wall and appeared to be suspended in air.

The overall feel was one of class and sophistication, and John was impressed. Something was odd, though. No one was seated at the receptionist's desk. Instead, a small bell sat by itself on the countertop. Bruce strode over and clapped his hand down on the bell, which responded with a resounding ding.

A few seconds later, a nice looking, well dressed man about 35 years old emerged from a hallway hidden behind the lettered wall. He smiled broadly as he extended his hand to Bruce.

"Bruce, my good man, how are you?" he asked. "It's been way too long since we got together. At least a week!"

Bruce laughed as he introduced John to Dave Barnett. Dave then led them to the hidden hallway behind the reception area and down a broad, carpeted corridor to a door at the end. The door opened to a covered breezeway, spanning a short distance between this building and another. They entered the next building, which was a spotlessly clean warehouse with vast, empty spaces.

"This is impressive. Everything looks so new and clean," John remarked. As he looked around, he thought, *But why is it so empty?*

As they walked around the warehouse, Dave explained the various types of medical equipment and supplies the company sold. They made their way back to the first building and Dave led them to a large conference room. Again, the décor and furnishings were rich and tasteful. Coffee paraphernalia and a plateful of cookies sat in the middle of the table. John was relieved to know the meeting would be spent in comfort, as he eyed the well-cushioned leather swivel chairs and refreshments.

Another man and a woman entered the room and waved to Bruce as they took their places at the table. Bruce introduced them.

"John, I'd like you to meet Dave's partners, Joe Smith and Diana Billings. Joe and Diana, this is John Clairren."

Greetings and handshakes were exchanged and they all seated themselves, passing around the coffee decanter and cookies.

Bruce began, "Dave, Joe and Diana are equal owners of Boorley Medical and I've worked with them for about a year now. I've asked them to meet with us today to share their story." He paused and looked expectantly around the table. "Who's going to start us off?"

Dave spoke up, "I'll start, Bruce." He looked directly at John and began his narrative.

"I guess I'll begin by telling you how we got involved with Boorley Medical in the first place. We all used to work on the same team at another company a number of years ago and became good friends in the process. It was a successful company and we liked our jobs, but we all had a strong desire to have our own businesses.

"Joe had talked to his dad at length about his desire to strike out on his own. When his dad heard Boorley Medical was for sale, he immediately called Joe. But Joe didn't believe he had the financial wherewithal at the time to buy a company, so he asked Diana and me if we'd be interested in buying it with him.

"Boorley distributes medical products and was started about 20 years ago. At the time it came up for sale, it was bringing in about $4.5 million a year. The owner, Ed Boorley, was motivated to sell because he wanted to retire and move to Arizona, so he wasn't asking a lot for the business. Just enough to give him a comfortable nest egg.

"After our due diligence review, we believed the price was reasonable and the company could be grown and sustained into the future. We got some good financing, resigned from our jobs and bought the operation.

"We felt it was best to keep the name Boorley Medical since the name carried a level of good will, so we didn't change it. We each had a special niche we could fill in running the company. I'm president and oversee sales. Joe has a background in finance, so he's our CFO. And since Diana was a mid-level manager at the old company, she took over general management."

Dave stopped to take a sip of coffee before continuing. "Have you ever heard the old expression about having champagne tastes and a beer pocketbook?"

John smiled and nodded his head.

"Well, having champagne tastes definitely describes the three of us in those early stages. We all had grandiose visions of the future— you know, the three wealthy business owners arriving in their sports cars, having all the perks of success. That sounded awfully good to us and I have to admit I was probably the worst of the three. I especially liked the idea of all the prestige."

"Oh, come on, Dave. We were all just as bad," Diana interjected as Joe nodded in agreement.

"Okay, we were all equally bad about it, but we really did want to make this company a huge success. We were moving along fine with the business just as we bought it. Same location, same size…and learning as we went. None of us had a background in medical supplies or distributing, so there was definitely a learning curve."

"Amen!" Joe exclaimed.

Dave took a deep breath and continued. "So now we come to the point where we started making extremely unwise decisions."

"What an understatement," Diana muttered under her breath. Then she declared forcefully, "We made some downright *stupid* decisions!"

"Yes, we did," Dave responded with a rueful smile. "A little more than two years ago, we thought we had hit a home run. We landed a client most business owners only dream of. They assured us they would be sending huge orders our way for a very long time. Not only that, but they promised to send us additional business from their affiliate companies. From all indications, the new orders would take us to over $7 million in revenue.

"Well, we felt as if we'd hit the jackpot in Las Vegas! I remember very clearly our 'victory dinner,' when we all took our spouses to an expensive restaurant to celebrate the new customer." Dave shook his head and smiled as the memories flooded back.

John was taking notes and looked up when Dave paused. "So what went wrong? It sounds like you were in very good shape at that point. What was the problem?"

"We were in good shape, or at least, we thought we were. We decided that with such a big customer promising us a huge amount of business, plus all its affiliates' business, we'd better step up." Dave took a blank piece of paper and drew the now familiar staircase diagram.

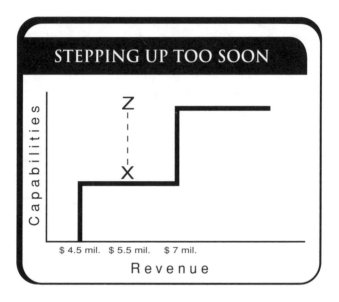

John looked over at Bruce and remarked, "Boy, that Step Dynamic drawing certainly gets around!"

Bruce nodded as Dave continued with the diagram, marking it with an X and a Z.

Dave looked at John. "You've obviously seen The Step Dynamic graph before. The X shows where we were located when we initially landed the new customer. The Z shows where we went when we stepped up. As you can see, the Z is not even on a step, which is bad. *That's* the problem, John." He turned to Joe and said,

"Why don't you pick up the story from here?"

"Glad to," responded Joe. "We thought we had landed a giant customer that would be bringing us a huge influx of orders and cash, and sending us additional business from its affiliates. In order to handle all the business we *thought* we were going to get, we spent a fortune stepping up.

"We moved into this facility, hired an interior decorator and got it all decked out. We wanted to look like a first-class operation, so we bought a lot of fancy new warehouse racks and shelves, and two brand new forklifts. We hired a couple of new salespeople, an office manager to oversee whatever an office manager is supposed to oversee, a receptionist, and some more people to work in the warehouse. We bought some new trucks, a fancy phone system and a bunch of computers that had to be networked."

Diana chimed in. "Don't forget the accounting software!"

"Oh yeah, let us not forget the software," Joe moaned. "We had been using off-the-shelf accounting software, which had always served us perfectly well. But we thought we were going to be inundated with all this new work and simply *had* to have software that would manage our warehouse and our accounting. It cost $100,000 when we bought it, thousands more for installation and training, and because it was so complicated, we had to hire an internal accountant to run it. Can you believe it?"

John gave a long whistle through his teeth. "Man, that's a lot of money for software!"

"We were caught up in the excitement of all the anticipated business growth, so we bought it. That's one of those 'unwise decisions' Dave mentioned. It could be a wise investment for some companies but we sure didn't need it. Everything might have worked out just fine if our wonderful new customer had followed through with all the hype and promises. We had never signed a contract and were relying on verbal assurances we were getting their business. And one day they simply disappeared."

"What do you mean they disappeared?" asked John.

"They didn't literally disappear," replied Joe. "They just stopped calling in orders. When we called their contact person to ask if anything was wrong, he told us they had found someone else they thought was better. We were floored because we had never seen it coming, so we decided to go up the ladder to try to salvage the relationship. We met with the company president to see if there was some way to continue to work with them. He wouldn't elaborate on the reason but told us the decision was final. We weren't going to get any more work from them or their affiliates."

"Oh crud!" moaned John.

"Oh crud, indeed. We were in a terrible bind because of all the money we'd spent buying stuff for the company to step up. Our old customers certainly didn't bring in enough to cover it all." Joe took a sip of his coffee and asked Diana to continue.

Diana nodded and began, "As you can imagine, we were pretty much in a state of panic that day. We had been sitting on a big magic carpet of anticipation and someone had just yanked the rug right out from underneath us. I can tell you, the bare floor didn't feel so good!"

"That must have been horrible," remarked John. "How did you survive?"

"Dave had heard about Bruce from an acquaintance; how he's retired but likes to spend his time consulting with business owners. Dave had never given Bruce much thought before. He never thought we'd need help from someone like Bruce. We tracked him down and he agreed to meet with us. He came out, toured the place and took tons of notes. Then he sat us all down and laid it out for us. He told us we had two choices."

John looked over at Bruce quizzically. "Two choices this time, eh? This morning it was four!"

"Yes, but these guys were in a bit of a tighter squeeze," countered Bruce.

"We were squeezed all right," admitted Diana. "Our situation nearly squeezed the life right out of this company! But we had those two options."

She held up a hand to illustrate her point by counting out fingers. "One, we could back up, shrink the operation and try to return to profitability by reducing our capabilities. Two, we could increase our sales to about the $7 million level that would allow us to pay for all the new capabilities. Those were our choices. Period."

"Man, those are both tough decisions," remarked John.

"You bet they are," Diana continued. "Let's say you have all this capability like we did and you want to back up. This means you've got to break your lease and move to smaller space. That can cause legal hassles since landlords generally don't like having broken leases. Then you've got all this used technology—computers, phone system, $100,000 software. Even if you're lucky enough to find someone to buy them from you, there's no way you'll ever come close to recouping what you spent.

"Our other choice was to dramatically increase our sales but that's not such an easy thing to do either. If it were, then every entrepreneur in this country would be wealthy. You don't just snap your fingers and have sales instantly appear."

"You sure don't," John agreed. "I still can't imagine how you managed to survive, given the magnitude of the problems you were facing."

"We hashed it all out with Bruce and determined our best course of action was to sell like crazy and try to get as much new business as we could. We let a bunch of people go: the warehouse guys, the new salespeople, the accountant, the office manager and, as you probably noticed, the receptionist." Diana gave John a wry smile.

"Since then we've been operating with a skeleton crew. The three of us knuckled down and have been answering phones, doing our own books, and putting in very long hours selling, selling and selling. In fact, we've spent so much time on airplanes we think of pretzels as a food group!"

Everyone grinned at Diana's joke and she continued, "It's been tough and quite a blow to our egos, but we're still here."

John was amazed they'd been able to pull it off and at how much the three owners were now doing in order to keep their business afloat. It seemed overwhelming. "Wow, I'm very impressed."

Dave took up the story again. "It's been hard work but we're finally pulling out of it and moving ahead steadily. It took about six months to rebuild sales to the break-even point and another six months to start making some okay profits. That's where we are today. Our sales are doing well, we're covering our bills and we have some profit left over." He paused and grinned. "*And* we've got a new receptionist starting next Monday so you won't have to ring the bell anymore."

Bruce turned to Dave. "After hearing their story, do you understand why they had the problems they encountered?"

"I think so. In their efforts to step up suddenly, they ended up way off The Step Dynamic staircase. When things didn't turn out as expected, they had far too many capabilities and huge expenses along with them. Correct?"

"That's right," answered Bruce. "They made a couple of big mistakes. They stepped up their capabilities too soon, before they had taken advantage of the capabilities they already had prior to the step-up. And although they couldn't foresee the other company would change its mind, they had never signed any kind of agreement and were stepping up based on promises.

"The danger with step-ups is everything usually happens in a very short time frame. More space and equipment are needed, more people have to be hired, maybe new software is installed…it all comes in a lump. If you end up having inadequate sales to cover the expenses, as these guys did, you're in a real bind."

Dave, Diana and Joe all nodded their heads simultaneously.

Bruce continued, "You noticed these guys only had two options, but Bob explained this morning he'd had four. Here's why there were only two this time. First, staying put isn't an option when you've stepped up too soon. You typically incur a great deal of expense when you step up your capabilities and if you try to stay where you are without having the sales volume to cover your costs, you'll end up in bankruptcy court.

"Second, another option Bob had that's missing in this case was selling his company. But it would have been virtually impossible here. No one in their right mind would have considered buying a company so obviously in the red.

"So, these guys did the only thing that made sense for their company and it worked for them. But it's been a long, hard road and they've worked their tails off to stay in business."

"I know I've worked mine off!" exclaimed Joe. He jumped up, twisted around and pointed at his backside. "See how flat it is?"

"Oh, please!" Diana exclaimed as everyone else shook their heads and chuckled.

Bruce stood and shook each of his hosts' hands. "Thank you for giving us your valuable time and for being willing to share your story so openly with John. You've given him a gift today that I hope will stay with him for a long time."

John reached to shake hands with each of them in turn, while echoing Bruce's appreciation. "Yes, thank you for your openness. I feel like I've just completed a college tutorial!"

Joe said, "Yeah, the College of Hard Knocks and Dumb Decisions!"

Dave accompanied Bruce and John to the front door. "Any time you have a question about anything we've discussed, John, feel free to call us. We owe Bruce a lot for helping us when he did and want to help wherever we can."

On the way back to John's office, he was quiet and reflective. Finally, Bruce broke the silence.

"So do you feel that your time today was well spent?"

"Oh, yeah. I feel very lucky to have a chance to learn from someone else's mistakes instead of charging ahead and making the same mistakes myself."

"Now you've learned what not do to and it's time to learn what some folks have done correctly. We'll do that tomorrow."

"That sounds great," said John as they pulled into his company's parking lot. "Hey, I've thanked everyone we've met with today, but I don't believe I've thanked you yet. Thanks for taking such an interest in my business and me. I really do appreciate it."

"You're very welcome. This type of consulting gives me great satisfaction and joy."

As John walked back to his office, tired but happy after his day of field trips, he wondered what tomorrow would bring.

Chapter Five

Moving Along the Step— Capitalizing on Your Capabilities

Although the downtown high-rise had been built in the 1920s, it was sleek, shiny and solid, boasting a façade of smooth, glistening black granite and silvery reflective windows. A bank took up the whole first floor. The upper floors housed primarily professional organizations: accountants, attorneys, a land trust, and this morning's destination, a marketing agency.

It was Friday morning, around 10:00. As John and Bruce disembarked from the elevator on the 17th floor, they were met by thick emerald green carpeting and wall paneling made of cherry wood. These imparted a feeling of rich warmth that said "tradition."

A pair of double doors with "Jaxton Marketing" printed in gold letters stood at one end of the elevator landing. The richly conservative look of the hallway was a dramatic contrast to what they saw as they pushed through those doors. It felt like a different world.

The emerald carpet merged into lime green walls. Sleek, black leather furniture was grouped around cube tables made of onyx and abstract paintings marched across the walls. A trendy young woman with spiked red hair and a long row of earrings running up each ear sat at the reception desk. Behind her was a clear glass wall. Through this wall, people were visible, scurrying around intensely.

"I'm Bruce Baxleigh and this is John Clairren. We're here to see Margaret and Tom," Bruce explained to the receptionist. "They're expecting us."

"Thank you. I'll ring back to them." The red haired woman punched a number into her desk phone and announced the guests. Then she smiled brightly at the two men and said, "They'll be right with you. Would you care for a latte?"

"Yes, please," Bruce responded.

"I'm more of a black coffee guy but, sure, why not?" answered John.

John had been busy poring over a glossy advertising magazine that occupied the glass topped coffee table. "Gosh, if these guys do anything like the ads in this magazine, they're really good," he remarked as Bruce handed him his latte.

"Oh yes, they're extremely talented at what they do. Trust me…you'll be amazed."

Their attention was diverted from the magazine when a handsome, 40-ish man and a dazzling blonde woman came out from behind the glass wall and greeted them warmly.

"Bruce, how wonderful to see you!" the woman exclaimed as she kissed his cheek. Then she turned to John. "And you must be John. Bruce has told us all about you. I'm Margaret Jaxton." She flashed John a startlingly white smile.

The man was equally welcoming, and gave John a strong handshake and warm smile. "I'm Tom Jaxton. We're glad to have the chance to meet with you, John. It's always fun to show off our operation and crow a little," he said.

"Well," Bruce said expansively as he spread his arms wide. "We're all together, so why don't you take us on a quick tour. We can get down to business right away so we don't take up too much of your time.

"You got it," said Tom. Turning to John, he said, "Follow me."

Bruce and John were led into the "guts" of the operation, peering into cubicles set about the perimeter of a large open space that was dotted with long tables. People seated in the cubicles were concentrating intently on their computer screens. As they walked along, Tom talked about different advertising campaigns the company had in the works and explained the various specialties of their employees. Then he led them out of the open area and into a conference room, which contained cushioned armchairs and a large screen at one end.

Margaret invited John and Bruce to be seated. As Tom made his way to a control panel on the end of the table, he announced, "Before we start our meeting, we'd like for you to see a short promotional video that will give John a better idea of what we do." Margaret switched off the lights as Tom punched buttons on the console, and the video began.

It lasted about ten minutes and included photos from a number of sleek and sophisticated advertising campaigns created by the firm. Once the video was over and the lights were turned up, John turned in his chair to face Margaret and Tom.

"I've seen several of these ads in magazines and I'm floored to learn your company created them!" he exclaimed. "I had never heard of your firm and certainly didn't realize someone in our town had this level of expertise. They're phenomenal!"

"Thanks, John," Tom responded with obvious pride as he rose from the control console. "We've got an extremely talented staff—young and dynamic, with fresh new ideas. In fact, Margaret and I are the old timers around here! We're very proud of our work. But we'll explain all that to you during our meeting. Let's go to my office."

He led them to an office that boasted floor-to-ceiling windows, a panoramic view and a comfortable seating area. With an exaggerated sweep of his arm, Tom offered John and Bruce seats on a sofa, while he and Margaret sat in armchairs facing them. John opened his leather satchel and extracted his notepad and pen, preparing to take notes.

Bruce began. "Tom and Margaret asked me to lead today's discussion, John, and they'll jump in with comments. But before we get into how The Step Dynamic worked for Jaxton Marketing, I'd like Margaret to explain the history of the company. Would you do that for us, Margaret?"

"Of course," she answered. "I'll start at the very beginning. Tom and I met at college, when we were both marketing majors at Northwestern University. We married right after graduation and took jobs with different companies. Tom went to work for a marketing firm and stayed there for seven years."

"That was great experience for me. I learned a lot," interjected Tom.

Margaret nodded and continued. "My first job was as public relations director for a Fortune 500 company that sold consumer foods; then I switched to a large ad agency. That was a bit awkward since we were working for competing companies, but Tom specialized in sports products and I primarily focused on high fashion, so it worked out okay. We had always intended to launch our own company someday, so we tried to learn as much as we could from our jobs.

"We saved as much money as possible and were finally able to start this company on a shoestring six years ago. In those days, we pretty much did everything ourselves. We could barely afford to pay ourselves salaries, so we lived in a very small apartment for a couple of years until business started picking up."

John looked around at the attractive office and commented, "Well, you've certainly come a long way since those days, haven't you? This looks like a first-class operation."

"Oh yes, we've come a very long way," answered Tom. "But it took a heck of a lot of hard work and planning on our part to get here. We badly wanted to be a major player in the marketing arena and we just kept growing the company until we ended up in this facility. However, we became leery of making bad decisions and ruining what we had worked so hard to build, so we brought Bruce in to help us strategically navigate this phase of our business."

"Bruce has definitely been our mentor," Margaret said enthusiastically, smiling broadly at Bruce. "He and my father have been friends for years. One day when we were chatting with Dad about our company and our hopes for the future, he said we really must sit down with Bruce and let him help us. So we did."

Tom continued. "After meeting with Bruce a number of times—just as you're doing—we had a pretty clear idea of what decisions we needed to make and when they should be made." He looked over at Bruce. "I think this is the part where you need to take over."

Bruce looked directly at John and began.

"By now you're well acquainted with The Step Dynamic diagram. You've seen it illustrated at the last two companies we've visited. Those companies were perfect examples of how things can go seriously wrong when you take your business off of the steps by making wrong decisions at the wrong time.

"In this case, I'm going to show you how Jaxton Marketing has used the principals of The Step Dynamic to its advantage. As Tom explained, they've experienced a number of growth spurts that have brought them to this point. And, I might add, they've done extremely well at handling their growth, as you can see from their operation. Today we're going to discuss the phase at which they're currently operating because they're a perfect example of the horizontal stage of The Step Dynamic."

Bruce took a legal pad from his leather folder and drew a close-up of one step on The Step Dynamic staircase diagram.

Pointing with his pen to the drawing, he continued. Jaxton Marketing had reached revenue of about $3.2 million. Tom and Margaret wanted to take advantage of all of their existing capabilities, so they timed their next step-up to occur about the time those capabilities were being maximized. Eighteen months ago they made that next step-up in capabilities, which put them at the Phase 1 position on the graph. As you can see, I've marked that 'Sales Focus.' So, John, why do you think it was most important for them to focus on sales after they completed the step-up?"

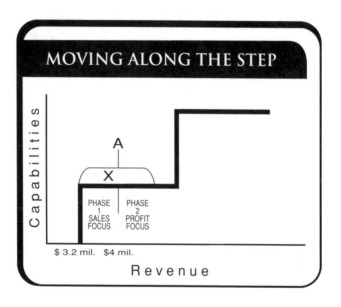

John knew the answer. "They needed more sales to generate the revenue to pay for all of the new capabilities."

"Absolutely correct," Bruce said. "The Step Dynamic is all about knowing how to make the right decisions at the right time. At Phase 1 on the step, you've got to focus the majority of your efforts on building sales to pay for the excess capabilities you've just added. Nothing else is as important at this stage, so it's imperative that you make sales and marketing your top priority."

"I thought all parts of a business were equally important," remarked John. "Don't the other parts suffer if you just zero in on sales?"

"Focusing on sales doesn't mean you don't take care of all the other parts of your business," Bruce answered. "But when you're building your plan and setting out your goals at this stage, your number one priority must be sales. Otherwise the operating costs of all the capabilities can sink you.

"Now, there's something I need to make clear. When you make your step-up in capabilities, you must be sure to include those capabilities necessary for a sales and marketing focus. That way you'll be adequately prepared when you reach Phase 1 on the step. For example, you need to have adequate salespeople and a marketing plan in place so that you're ready to go. Tom and Margaret did exactly that and were able to direct their focus to sales and marketing when they reached Phase 1."

Bruce paused and looked at Margaret and Tom. "Would you two say that increasing sales was a difficult thing for you to do at that time?"

Margaret looked over at Tom and

answered tentatively, "Well, I wouldn't say it was difficult in the respect that we're both comfortable with selling. But it did require a great deal of work on our part. A lot of intensity for awhile."

"But it was well worth the effort," added Tom. "We did work like the dickens for awhile but it was an extremely smooth journey along that phase of the step. Mainly because we had prepared for the step-up. Capabilities were in place so we could focus on marketing and generating sales. And that sales focus brought in a lot of new revenue."

Bruce nodded his head in agreement. "This may seem like a simple concept but it's one that's often overlooked: the area where you focus your time and energy is the one that will get results. Again, doing the right thing at the right time. Once you've started to capitalize on your capabilities by bringing in sales, you should start to see your profits grow."

Directing his attention to the step he'd drawn, Bruce aimed his pen at a point about a third of the way along the horizontal line of the step. "At Phase 2, you've gotten the sales to support the capabilities which, in Tom and Margaret's case, was about $4 million in sales. Now your priorities should start to shift to a focus on profitability. Again, you don't want to neglect the other areas of your business. But now your focus must be on things that increase profitability, such as increasing employee efficiency, improving technology utilization and improving the workflow process. Tom, why don't you take over?"

"Okay," answered Tom. "We reached the point where we had strong sales, so now we re-prioritized our goals to put time and effort into maximizing our profitability."

"Could you explain more about what that actually involved in your company?" asked John.

"Sure. Bruce made it clear we needed to capitalize on the capabilities we already had before even considering a step-up." Tom paused for a moment to collect his thoughts before continuing. "For example, we began focusing on doing things more efficiently, such as figuring out how we could complete projects in less time by improving workflow. That would allow us to handle more projects without a big jump in personnel. We also reviewed all of our clients to determine whether we needed to change the way we were billing them. In several cases, we increased prices for our work."

Margaret added, "Another way we've increased our efficiency is with our design software. It's quite sophisticated and we weren't fully utilizing it, so we're getting additional training. As a result, we'll be able to increase what we do for our clients and add a few new services. And next month we're going to start some focus groups to get a clearer understanding of our 'A' clients and how we can better serve them. So, as we continue to move along this phase of the step, profits will continue to increase."

"I'm getting it," John said. "You don't stop selling or providing great service, but the highest priority for your time at this point is looking at ways to increase your profits. Other areas of your business have to take second place to focusing on profitability and I think I know why."

"Why do you believe that's the case?" Bruce asked.

"Well, I can think of two reasons. First, as you move down the path, you know another step is on the way if you plan to continue growing. If you haven't earned enough money to build up reserves, you won't have the financial resources to pay for the next step."

"Very good, but what else?" Bruce gestured for John to continue.

"Second, if you increase your profits, you can invest time and money in things that will support even greater profitability. On the other hand, if you didn't have the additional money, you couldn't do those things because you'd only be squeaking by."

"Exactly," Bruce replied.

"Today we're in a comfortable place," said Margaret. "We've given ourselves nice pay raises and recently bought a home in Cedar Heights. Not that we relaxed or took our eyes off the business," she added earnestly. "But by handling our growth in the right way, we've got time and money for ourselves and the business. I think many entrepreneurs probably only dream of reaching this place, but Bruce showed us how to achieve it." She was obviously proud of their accomplishments and smiled broadly.

Tom chimed in. "I agree. In fact, I think of all the stages you can be on The Step Dynamic graph, we're currently at the most comfortable position. Running this place is easy, primarily because we don't have cash flow problems or a lot of other issues. Of course, we've had problems crop up from time to time, but they haven't seemed overwhelming and we've simply dealt with them. And for the first time in our married life, we're able to work a reasonable number of hours each week so we actually see each other away from the office!"

Margaret winked at Tom. "Oh yes, it's been nice! Seeing your spouse across a conference table just isn't the same as getting to spend time together at home once in awhile."

"Frankly, I'm amazed you two are able to work together so well," John responded. "I don't know many married couples who could pull it off. My wife and I would probably kill each other!"

"Well, it does have its challenges. On a few occasions, Tom and I have bet each other that we could have a romantic dinner out without once discussing business. But one of us always goofs and blurts out something related to the office." Margaret pealed with laughter. "We're really quite pathetic! One time we sat in a lovely restaurant for twenty minutes without saying a word!"

Tom reached over to pat Margaret's hand. "That's okay, Sweetheart. At least we never have to ask how each other's day went. We already know because we both have the same day!"

Bruce chuckled and turned to John. "Are you seeing how smoothly the growth process can run if you do it correctly?" When John nodded, Bruce continued. "Tom and Margaret are looking at the next phase of their business, but we're not going into detail about that right now. The point of this visit was to illustrate what should happen in the first two phases of the horizontal portion of a step according to The

Step Dynamic. Jaxton Marketing is a perfect example of that."

Bruce stood up and stretched. "Maggie, my darling, and Tom, thanks for giving us your time today. I can't begin to tell you how proud I am of you two."

Margaret stood up and kissed Bruce on the cheek. "We're always glad to spend time with you and we're proud to show off our 'baby' anytime you want us to."

"Well, I've got to say, this has been the most entertaining 'classroom experience' I've ever had," exclaimed John. "I'm so glad I had the chance to meet you, and I appreciate your taking time to share your story."

As they rode down in the elevator, John remarked, "That was great! I'm learning a ton of stuff I'd never thought about before."

"So these field trips aren't so bad, eh?"

"No, I like them. You know, the last time I went on a field trip was in fifth grade and I dropped ice down Debbie Miller's dress. It was actually quite educational because I learned a seventy-pound girl can knock an eighty-pound boy flat on his back on a sidewalk! These lessons are considerably more pleasant to learn!"

"Good grief, I hope so! Let's grab lunch and move on to our next learning experience. But I'll be watching you and the ice."

Chapter Six

The Step Up— Taking Your Business to the Next Level

After a quick lunch, during which they discussed John's love of fishing and Bruce's passion for skiing, the two men climbed back into Bruce's car. It had heated up considerably as it sat in the morning sun.

Rolling down the windows to let in some cooler air, Bruce asked, "How did you like Margaret and Tom? Aren't they special people?"

John was still amazed to have learned "real" people, as opposed to a New York agency, had produced the glossy ads he'd seen in magazines. "Oh, I'd definitely say they're special. I can't see how you're possibly going to top them."

"I don't know if you'll think our next entrepreneur exactly tops anyone, but I do think you're going to be glad you met him."

"Hey, I just thought of something. Am I going to be expected to take any kind of test when this is all over?"

Bruce stroked his chin in a villainous gesture. "A test! What a wonderful idea!" As John made a loud moan, Bruce continued, "Not exactly a test but I do plan to spirit you away to my home for a debriefing. Are you game?"

"Oh, why not? I've already put myself at your mercy these last two days and you haven't killed me off yet," John shot back.

Bruce laughed, and then became serious. "I thought I'd fill you in a bit on our next meeting while we're on our way. The man we're going to see is an extremely interesting fellow. He's kind of eccentric and absolutely brilliant, but he's also a heck of a nice guy. His name is Bradford Bellweather, if you can believe it."

"No way!"

"Dead serious. That's really his name."

"Good grief, no wonder he's eccentric with a handle like that! What kind of business does he run?"

"Brad invented a process for creating precision ceramic parts for the aerospace industry. He started out in a laboratory in his basement at home many years ago and now has a sizable plant."

"He sounds like a real life Mr. Wizard."

"That's pretty much who he is. If I tell you how he likes to come up with ideas for inventions you'll never believe me, but it's absolutely true."

John was intrigued. "All right, tell me. I'm prepared for anything."

"He sits in his hot tub at home."

"So? What's the big deal?"

"He sits in his hot tub at home. Underwater on the floor. With a snorkel."

"No way! I don't believe it," John retorted. "Nobody's that weird!"

"Oh, yes they are!" Bruce laughed. "That's exactly how Brad likes to think through his inventions. He says the water muffles the sound and all he can hear is his own heartbeat. He insists it's great for concentration."

John shook his head in amazement. "Oh well, whatever works!"

When they pulled into the parking lot at Bellweather Industries, John was immediately struck by the size of the place. He had been expecting a mid-sized light industrial building but was met with a massive structure.

"Whew! This guy may be a little unusual, but he obviously knows what growing a company is all about," he ventured.

"Oh yes," Bruce responded. "As I said, he started out in his basement and grew the company to this size in about 12 years, so he definitely knows how to grow."

The two men entered the building through double doors and crossed a sizeable entrance hall to reach a long, marble-topped counter. A pleasant looking, middle-aged woman was seated behind it and looked up from her work to smile at them warmly. After they signed the visitor's log, she picked up the phone, dialed a number and announced, "Mr. Bellweather, Mr. Baxleigh and Mr. Clairren are here to see you."

They seated themselves on a comfortable leather sofa. After about five minutes (just when John was thinking he could do some serious sleeping on that sofa), a tall man, who appeared to be in his sixties, joined them. A prominent clump of gray hair stuck up directly in the middle of his head, giving him a very odd appearance. He was wearing a white lab coat and huge, black-rimmed glasses, making him look like the stereotypical mad professor. As

Bruce had described, he certainly looked eccentric.

Greetings were exchanged and Brad Bellweather led his guests up two flights of stairs to a large conference room on the third floor. One full wall of the room was comprised of windows overlooking the manufacturing plant below. He walked to the window and looked down, an expression of satisfaction on his face.

"John, welcome to my world."

John surveyed the bustling activity below and felt somewhat like a Peeping Tom as he watched the employees at their tasks. The work area was starkly white and spotlessly clean. The equipment, with its sleek lines and flashing lights, made the area resemble something from a science fiction movie. All of the workers wore what appeared to be a type of white space suit, with their heads incased in hoods. Some kind of clear panel covered their faces.

"Why are they all wearing those get-ups?" John asked. "They look like they'd be extremely hot."

"Actually, the room is tightly temperature-controlled and would feel quite chilly if one were wearing street clothes, so the protective suits are very comfortable. It's called a clean room. The parts we produce are so precise that even a microscopic speck of dust could throw off measurements, so the air is carefully filtered and no one is allowed in wearing street clothes."

"Fascinating!" John replied.

Brad turned from the window and offered his guests seats at the conference table. A nice selection of beverages was grouped at one end of the table, so they all helped themselves and began their meeting.

"John, Brad is going to tell you about his experience with our next topic, which is preparing to step up and what it involves. As you can see, he has stepped up quite well."

Brad took over. "As you may have guessed, I am a proponent of Bruce's Step Dynamic principles. You may not know this, but Bruce is my brother-in-law."

John's eyes shot open in surprise and the other men smiled.

"Bruce and I have known each other for some 30 years. I witnessed Bruce's own experiences with business ownership with great interest, although he didn't share his theories about The Step Dynamic until he had them nailed down."

"I didn't want my brilliant brother-in-law to have any more reason to think he was superior. I wanted to have my ducks in a row!" Bruce said with a grin.

Brad continued. "This company had gone through a number of relatively small growth spurts, some of which I handled well and some of which I mishandled, but the business managed to survive. However, four years ago, when sales had grown to about $10 million, we reached a point at which I believed we were facing significant growth issues. I began consulting with Bruce. He was still working full-time in his own company and had only shared his Step Dynamic theory with a couple of other people. So you might say I was one of his first test subjects."

Standing up and walking to the expansive white board on the wall opposite the windows, Brad adopted a professor's demeanor. He picked up a marker and drew The Step Dynamic diagram. He placed a large B on a spot along one of the steps and wrote "4 years ago" underneath it. On the step above, he wrote another B with the word "today."

"This is the point where my company was operating when I consulted Bruce. For this meeting, however, we're going to pretend you're the business owner in question. Let's say you've reached this point, which is about two-thirds of the way along the step. Your sales volume and capabilities are in sync, your business is humming along nicely, but now you have to make some important decisions about growth. Can you tell me what your options might be?"

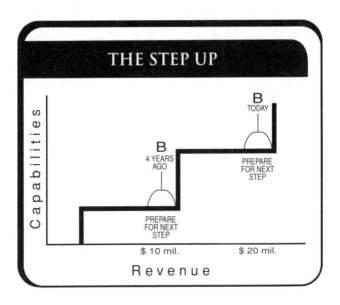

John studied the diagram thoughtfully, then ventured a guess. "I believe I'd have a couple of choices here. I could either be content with the size of my company and stay put for awhile, or I would need to think about stepping up again."

"Bravo! As long as your competitors or advancing technology aren't breathing down your neck, you can afford to stay put. However, if stepping up is necessary to keep up with the competition, as in my case, or if you want to take your business to the next level, you need to start thinking about stepping up. That's the critical thing at this stage: you've got to think."

He continued, "This is the point at which you plan your growth, and determine where you want to be and what needs to be done in order to get there. You have to ask yourself strategic questions. What increased capabilities will you need? What financing will be necessary to achieve your goal? What staffing will be required to operate the larger company? Will you need to implement additional systems and controls to prevent problems such as theft? Since a major step-up will involve potential changes in all parts of the business at about the same time, it's critical to have your strategy planned or you'll have problems in the future."

John paused in his note taking and remarked, "That's a lot to have to deal with all at one time, especially if you're trying to handle all the day-to-day parts of running your business at its existing level."

Brad nodded in agreement. "It is a lot. Commitment and self-discipline are required on your part, but the end result will be worth it. You'll have a much smoother transition as you step up, and operating your business will ultimately be easier. You can get yourself into a very difficult situation if you step up your capabilities without first doing your homework."

Bruce had listened quietly but, turning to John, he entered the conversation. "Remember our trip to the two companies yesterday? One was an example of not stepping up and overshooting the company's capabilities. The other was an example of stepping up too soon. Brad's business is a perfect example of the correct way to do it, by making the right decisions at the right time. He put a great deal of thought and effort into what a step-up would require, what would need to be accomplished and a timeline for when things should be done. Brad is a brilliant engineer, but he's also an astute businessman."

Brad bowed his head modestly in reaction to the praise. "Thank you, Bruce, but I don't believe I could have stepped up successfully without your input. You're right—it did take a lot of thought and effort. I did all of the strategizing and made informed, sound decisions. Now we're outgrowing this facility and preparing for the next step-up."

John looked up from his notes. "I have a question. You mentioned needing to keep up with competition but I thought you had a unique process. Why would you have competition?"

"Everyone has competition sooner or later. In technology, new products and processes are invented all the time. I became aware of at least two firms that had developed products and processes to compete with mine. Of course, I firmly believe my product is better than theirs, but you can't always rely on the consumer to know the difference. I knew the competition had the potential to take over my market if I didn't act.

"Part of my research involved asking myself some probing questions. Such as, whether I had the knowledge and skills to run a company of the size you see today, or whether I needed to hire senior management. In making a list of my skill set and natural abilities, I realized I'm good at looking at the big picture and creating new products, but not at running the day-to-day operations required by a larger business.

"Therefore, one of my first step-up activities was hiring a top-notch general manager. My time was then freed to focus on my strongest area of natural ability, which is working in the lab on product development and testing. We also significantly increased our staffing by hiring both administrative people and plant workers. We added entire departments, such as human resources and accounting, and implemented more stringent systems and controls with sophisticated reporting methods."

John shook his head. "It all seems pretty overwhelming to me."

Bruce spoke up. "John, you've told me you envision your own company growing substantially at some point in the future. It's important to understand that if you make a decision to step up, you don't have to do it all yourself. You can hire people to help you. Bring in contractors and consultants if necessary. It doesn't have to be overwhelming, but it does have to be strategic and effective. Again, making the right decisions at the right time.

"One reason it takes so much advance planning is many of the necessary tasks can't be completed overnight. For instance, stepping up costs money and you can't just snap your fingers and have financing materialize. It takes time to prepare a financing package for your proposed lender, and more time for the lender to approve your loan.

"If you need additional space, which you most likely will once you add employees and production capabilities, you'll have to spend time looking for a suitable location. Then you'll need to negotiate a lease, arrange for leasehold improvements and so on. And it takes time to hire the right people, and put new systems and controls in place.

"Brad's sales are now at around $20 million, so he's preparing to step up again. Adequate preparations for a step-up usually take six months to a year. If you get in a rush and don't do your homework, you won't be ready and can get into trouble. The bottom line is you have to see a step-up coming and prepare for it. You will need to allot a certain percentage of your focus to the step-up process, aside from day-to-day activities. Make it a priority."

"Bruce, what if I do all of my homework and decide I'm just not cut out for running a larger company?" asked John.

"If you've determined your existing business won't become obsolete because of advancing technology or get blown out of the water by competition, then it's probably safe to stay put. Another option is to consider selling. Maybe you'll decide it's time to get out of the business altogether, which is certainly a viable option."

Bruce stood and stretched. "Can you think of any more questions, John?"

"Not at the moment," John answered before turning to thank his host. "Brad, you've given me a lot to think about today and I appreciate your willingness to do this. It's obvious you've done things the right way and you can certainly be proud of what you've accomplished here."

"It's been my pleasure, John. Now you should make my brother-in-law take you somewhere more relaxing for your debriefing session."

"That's exactly what's planned," Bruce assured him. "We're heading up to the house now. Would you like to come with us?"

"I'd join you if I could get away for the afternoon, but I'm in the middle of an experiment. Another time."

"Okay, another time," answered Bruce, as he patted Brad on the shoulder. Turning to John he said, "Let's go, John. It's time for your debriefing session!"

Chapter Seven

Success Equals Making the Right Decisions at the Right Time

As they drove away from the Bellweather parking lot, John remarked, "What an interesting man! You know, the thing that's made these past two days the most enjoyable for me has been the variety. The different personalities and talents of the people I've met have been fascinating."

"They're different, all right. That's one of the reasons I love doing this consulting. I've met so many intriguing business owners along the way and they're a diverse group. From the innovative entrepreneur to the plumber who inherited his business from his father; from the guy with a Ph.D. to the one with 'street smarts'; from people who launched companies while still in their twenties to those who waited until they were 60—each one has taught me something different."

"I'll bet they have."

"You can't stereotype successful entrepreneurs. However, they must first have the desire and willingness to get the job done. Then the key is knowing where to focus their energies as their business grows."

"Which is where The Step Dynamic comes in," added John.

"Absolutely! Now we need to debrief from our field trips. Can you give me a recap of what you've learned in the last two days?"

John had thought of almost nothing else since starting out the previous day. "First, I learned that every business owner should meet Bruce Baxleigh!"

Bruce was pleased with the compliment. "I don't see how I could possibly fit them all into my schedule, but I do appreciate the recommendation. What else did you learn?"

"I learned that I wasn't as crazy as I thought after all. I had sought growth in my company but when it happened, my life got really tough. I thought I must be seriously deficient somehow. It was good to discover other people have experienced some of the same things. But I mainly learned that business growth is a good thing if it's handled properly."

"Okay. What else?"

"It basically boils down to making the right decisions at the right time."

"Can you give me an example?"

"Well, for one thing, you don't want to step up your capabilities sooner than you need to or you'll end up with huge expenses you can't afford to maintain."

"Good. Keep going."

"I learned that there are stages—or steps—involved in business growth and I need to watch for four critical places involving those steps."

"That's correct. What else?"

John thought for a few moments. "If I believe my company is close to needing to step up, then I've got to prepare for it. But I can't step up too early, nor should I wait too long to prepare for the next step-up. It's a matter of timing and understanding where my business is at any point in time so I can stay focused on the right things."

"You've definitely got a handle on The Step Dynamic, John. Do you have any questions?"

"Yes I do. I think I understand how and why The Step Dynamic principles work, and I know timing is important. But how am I supposed to know where my business is located in relation to the steps at any given time? I'm still not clear about that part."

"Perfect! That's exactly what I was looking for. When we get up to my house, we'll go over that while we have some refreshments and unwind a bit. How does that sound?"

"Perfect! That's exactly what *I* was looking for!"

Bruce's house was perched high on a hillside, accessed by a winding road through thickly forested acreage. The drive up to the house had been impressive enough, but the palatial house was even more so.

Bruce was clattering about in the kitchen, putting together drinks and snacks while John stood in the great room. He felt dwarfed by the towering moss rock fireplace that soared along one wall, and the sheer size of the room. *This is quite a house,* he thought.

As he waited for Bruce, John examined the family pictures arranged on a table. Most included children in various stages of growth, but one small, slightly grainy, black and white photograph caught his attention. It revealed a smiling young couple, holding hands and sitting on the floor of what appeared to be a sparsely furnished room.

At that moment, Bruce returned carrying a tray with wine, bottled water, cheese and crackers. "Ah, I see you've met Donna. Her hair is a bit more gray than it was in that photo but she's just as lovely."

John turned to look at Bruce and nodded. "She's beautiful. You both look very young in this picture."

Taking the frame from John's hand, Bruce smiled as he reminisced. "Yes, we were barely 20 years old. We were newlyweds and had just moved into our first place. Would you believe, that entire apartment wasn't much bigger than the walk-in closet we have now! That was almost 50 years ago."

"You've certainly come a long way since then!" John said as he looked appreciatively around the room. "It's obvious you've accumulated material wealth but I can't help thinking about the valuable relationships you've built. Everyone I met on our field trips obviously thinks very highly of you."

"I've definitely been fortunate to have those relationships. And I've been extremely blessed in my business. I think one of the greatest blessings has been learning from business failure and then applying those lessons to my last company. I firmly believe business owners can achieve great success if they know how to grow their companies correctly. On that note, let's go outside and continue our debriefing."

Bruce led the way through French doors onto a wraparound deck that offered a panoramic view of the city far below. The Colorado air was crisp and clean, and sweetly perfumed with pine. John breathed in deeply as he took a seat at a long patio table and looked at his splendid surroundings. "Bruce, this is magnificent."

"Isn't it, though? I always say God must be quite an artist to have created such beauty." After spreading the refreshments on the table and taking his seat, Bruce picked up the yellow legal pad he'd carried out on the tray and quickly sketched out The Step Dynamic diagram.

"Now, to continue with our debriefing. Your question in the car was how to know where a business is located in relation to The Step Dynamic at any given time. It requires a thorough, honest evaluation, which was my first task when I started working with each of the companies we visited. Let's look at each of those companies again, starting with the two problem companies we saw yesterday.

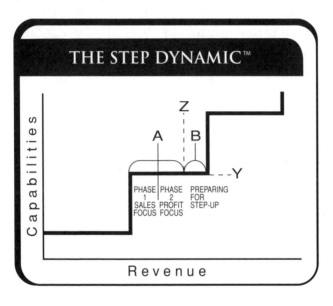

"Our first example of how not to grow was Bob's company, Pryce Concrete. It had landed in a Y position on The Step Dynamic graph." He looked up at John and asked, "Do you remember the major problem that company had encountered?"

"Yes, they had gotten more sales volume than their capabilities could handle. They had been completely overwhelmed."

"That's right. If your sales volume has blown past your capabilities, you feel overwhelmed by the entire business. Your capabilities are maxed out. Things you had control over when you were a smaller company are no longer working as they once did. You're constantly putting out fires. Problems you didn't have before, such as issues related to customer service and quality, are popping up on a constant basis.

"Things are falling through the cracks. You find yourself working more hours but still can't find the time to do business planning or correct what's wrong. Eventually, you and others in your company will burn out. Your profits will probably start to decrease despite the increased sales. Everything is being done in crisis mode."

"What about the Z position on the diagram?" John asked. "Boorley Medical had excess capabilities because they stepped up too soon. What are the signs of having stepped up too soon?"

"The best way I can put it is that you would have too much of everything except sales and cash," Bruce replied. "If your company has excess capabilities, you can find yourself drowning from the expense of those capabilities. Machinery sits idle. Office equipment is underutilized. There is too much space in the office, the shop…everywhere.

"The technology you're using may be overkill for the sales volume. The systems and controls are taking too much time for the value you're getting at this level of sales. You might have employees with skills significantly higher than what you need, so you'll be wasting money paying for overqualified people or underutilized staff.

"There is simply way too much of everything and, as a consequence, you lose money. Getting back to break-even would take a significant increase in sales."

John thought for a moment. "The folks at Boorley explained that they based their decisions on something they *thought* would occur and spent a fortune increasing their capabilities before they actually had the sales in hand. They stepped up too soon."

"That's right," Bruce replied.

"Well, it wouldn't involve a step-up, but couldn't a company find itself in the same type of situation—in the Z position—if it suddenly lost established customers?"

"Oh, yes. It's not the same as The Step Dynamic principle of stepping up too soon, but a sudden drop in revenue can certainly put a company in a position of having excess capabilities. In that case, the choices are the same—back up or sell like crazy."

Bruce selected a slice of cheese, crossed his legs and leaned back in his chair. "So, after all you've learned, do you see your company in either of those positions?"

"Yeah. My company is definitely at a Y point." John paused and chuckled. "I grew up in the South and we had a saying that kind of sums up my problem."

"What's that?" Bruce asked, intrigued.

"'Don't let your alligator mouth overload your hummingbird rear'! I've been telling my customers, 'Oh sure, we can do that,' when we were no more capable of filling those huge orders than my three-year old is capable of running the Boston Marathon."

Bruce broke out laughing. "I've never heard the alligator saying before, but it's a great one to describe having your sales blow past your capabilities. I'll remember it!"

John continued, "My biggest complaint in life lately has been feeling as though my business is running my life. I want to get back to the point where I'm in control and running *it*."

"How do you envision yourself achieving that?"

"I can clearly see I'm going to have to pull back and regroup before taking on the kind of sales volume we've been getting. We're simply in over our heads and our capabilities are inadequate. I never realized it before."

"Good observation," said Bruce. "I think you're definitely on the right track. Now let's revisit the two companies we saw who had handled their growth in a healthy manner. Jaxton Marketing represented the A position on The Step Dynamic graph. Do you have any questions about that situation?"

"Yes I do," John answered. "Of course, if you had just stepped up you would know it, but how would you know whether you had stepped up at the right time?"

"That's an excellent question. If you've stepped up at the right time, you're in the Phase 1 position on the step. You obviously have more capacity but it doesn't seem like overkill. You probably hired new employees with greater skills, but there are many things for them to do that will take advantage of those skills. You may still be going through some learning curves with the systems and controls, but it's obvious why they're needed.

"After stepping up, you might not be operating at break-even, but it wouldn't take a significant increase in sales to bring you to the break-even point. If the step-up was completed properly, everything is in place and the organization's top priority is adding revenue.

"Once your sales are producing a solid profit, which is usually about 30 to 40 percent of the way along the step, you can move on to the next phase. At Phase 2, you shift to focusing on the profitability of the business. In this phase, the business should be operating fairly smoothly. Profits should be good; and while there will always be issues, most should not be significant. At this point, it's best to make profitability the top priority. A business in this stage should be using its capabilities to find new ways to improve its bottom line."

"I can see that Jaxton Marketing is doing that," John commented. "They've made good decisions. They had made a step-up and, at that point, their first priority was obtaining sales. Now they're focused on maximizing profit without exceeding their capabilities. But they're not so excited about the success they've already experienced that they're rushing to step up their capabilities again."

"That's right," Bruce replied. "They're a prime example of making the right decisions at the right time."

John thought for a moment before asking his next question. "When we visited

Bellweather today, Brad explained they're at the B position on The Step Dynamic diagram. Could you explain further what a company preparing to step up would look like?"

"Sure. In Brad's case, he reached a point at which he knew his company had to grow to survive. He realized he was getting close to his capabilities being maximized. He did his homework, made some extremely wise decisions and stepped up. Now he's planning for his next step-up. He's building all the pieces he needs, so when he gets there he'll have everything in place.

"If your business is at this stage you start feeling that its capabilities are getting maxed out. You've done all you can at Phase 2 to get the most you can from your capabilities but they're reaching their limits. It's possible the people you have on staff won't be qualified to handle a larger business, and you can see that people with greater or different skills will be needed.

"You recognize that your existing systems, controls and technology will soon become ineffective and could even fail if much more sales volume is added. You start running out of places to put people in the current space. Your equipment, whether it's printing presses or office equipment, will soon become inadequate. Those are the types of things to look for."

"Is there an average amount of time after a step-up before you should plan for another one?" John asked.

"A step-up usually occurs when you have used up about 85 to 90 percent of your capabilities. In fast growing companies this could happen in a year but in some cases it takes many years before the need to step up."

"What's the best way to prepare for the step-up?"

"Since the business should be operating smoothly, the focus of key management needs to shift to planning for the step. You have to answer two questions. First, if you were at the higher level of sales, what would the company look like? You need to formulate a clear vision of your company at that size. Second, if your company reaches that level, what will you need to operate effectively? What capabilities will be needed in all areas of the business—sales, marketing, operations, customer service, technology, systems and controls, employees, space, equipment and so on."

"Not to mention money, right?" John added.

"Absolutely! Once you determine the level to which you want to take the company and what capabilities will be needed to achieve that level, you need to figure out how much money it will require. This can come from your cash reserves, by borrowing money, or from outside capital, but it's important to be sure you will have enough money. Otherwise, you'll experience cash flow problems."

"I learned two things from Brad: you need to do it right and the process of stepping up takes a lot of work," admitted John. "It sure sounds like he knows how to do it successfully."

"Brad is a brilliant businessman and he has definitely figured out how to grow his business the right way." Bruce smiled and added, "The family has always thought Brad was a bit of an odd duck but now he's a very wealthy odd duck! Actually, he's a fine man and I couldn't respect him more. It's wonderful to see the way he's built such a successful company."

John had another important question. "If a company were to buy new trucks or hire more employees, would that be considered stepping up?"

"Unless it was an extremely small company, that would be unlikely. For most businesses, it would simply be adding resources. In a step-up, as I define it, capabilities are added to the point that the whole business changes."

"Are there ways to make a step-up without taking on so much risk?"

"Oh, there are some ways but there are always trade-offs when you reduce risk," Bruce answered. "For example, instead of hiring permanent staff you could use contractors. But contractors would cost more than employees. Instead of signing a five-year lease for new space, you might negotiate temporary space. But a temporary lease would likely cost far more per month than you would pay for the five-year lease. These would only be temporary fixes since you'd eventually need permanent space and employees anyway."

Another question occurred to John. "Are there ever instances where it's impossible to step up?"

"I don't know if business growth is ever impossible but there are definitely instances where it would be more challenging." Bruce paused to collect his thoughts. "Here's an example. Say you own a fencing company in a small town. You could certainly reach a market saturation point and not realistically be able to step up so long as you confined your operation to that town. But you might consider geographic expansion to another location."

"That makes sense." John said. "What would happen if you were preparing to step up and got most of it right, but not everything? What if you didn't get all the money you needed? Or suppose you failed to build adequate systems and controls, or didn't have a qualified person in a critical position? How would that work?"

"What a great question!" Bruce answered. "Imagine that the step is not fully built; in other words, you didn't properly build up capabilities. This would mean your step wouldn't be flat. Instead, it would feel like running up a hill versus running along a flat road. The missing capabilities would continue to create problems in the business and you couldn't progress smoothly until you corrected the situation."

John ventured, "The folks at Jaxton Marketing said it was possible to focus on sales at the right time because all of their capabilities had been in place. But if they had been missing capabilities, their focus would have been diverted from sales because they would have been forced to spend their time correcting problems. Is that right?"

"Yes, that's correct." Bruce stood and walked over to the deck railing. "I believe you have a clear understanding of how and why

The Step Dynamic works. But can you think of anything we haven't covered these last two days?"

"Yes, something very important. What do I owe you?"

"I'm very glad you asked because I love getting paid. But as I said in the beginning, you don't owe me anything unless you feel this has been time well spent."

"Oh, it's definitely been time well spent," insisted John. "So what do I need to pay you for your time?"

"I'd like a commitment from you that at some point in the future I could bring a business owner to your place. You would teach him or her what you've learned about The Step Dynamic."

John waited for Bruce to continue with a price but when Bruce only smiled and said nothing further, he was amazed. "That's all?"

"That's all! I may be giving you a call in six months or so. Now, let's go inside to my study and I'll show you *my* trophy trout!"

Chapter Eight

Postscript

John sat at the conference table at Clairren Security, reflecting over the eight months that had elapsed since his field trips with Bruce Baxleigh. He mentally counted off the changes he'd seen, both in his business and his personal life.

After learning about The Step Dynamic, he'd been convinced that his company had overshot the step. He had decided to back up and regroup to get things under control. Sure, certain parts of the process had been tough, but Bruce had helped him with decision-making and now the company was back on track and running smoothly. He was currently in the process of preparing for a step-up in capabilities and was doing his homework. He felt confident about the future of Clairren Security.

Now that his business was under control, the overwhelming stress he'd felt eight months ago was gone. He felt better, looked healthier and life was fun again. He had just returned from a weeklong fishing trip in Alaska with Dave Johnson and, oh, the salmon they'd caught!

He was actually working reasonable hours these days and had more time for his family. *Karen doesn't refer to me as "Old What's His Name" anymore*, he thought as he laughed softly to himself.

A tap on the door interrupted his thoughts. The door opened slightly and Bruce's head appeared. Jumping to his feet, John walked over to greet his friend as Bruce entered the room, bringing another man with him.

"Hi Bruce! It's great to see you. And you must be Chuck."

"It's great to see you too, John." Bruce turned to the tall man at his side. "Chuck Milton, this is John Clairren. I think you'll enjoy hearing his story."

Did you recognize someone in this book? Maybe yourself?

♦ Do you want to create excellence in your company?

♦ Are you interested in achieving greater success as you grow your business?

♦ Are you finding that business growth is a struggle and you need better solutions?

♦ Do you want to take control of your growing company?

♦ Do you have a friend, acquaintance or client struggling with business growth issues?

We'd like to help you!

At BusinessTruths® Consulting, Inc., we're passionate about entrepreneurs and the companies they create. We offer a number of services and resources to help you successfully grow your company, build the business of your dreams, and create a company that will serve as a vehicle to achieve your personal goals.

Consulting Services: BusinessTruths® Consulting, Inc. works with privately-held companies of all sizes and industries. We can help you with strategic and business planning, growth issues, business assessment, and/or preparation for sale of your company. Contact us or visit our website at **www.BusinessTruths.com** to learn more about our consulting services.

Complimentary E-Newsletter: Subscribe to our free e-newsletter, *BusinessTruths® Monthly*, by visiting www.businesstruths.com/newsletter/ index.htm. This publication provides valuable information on a variety of timely business topics, including growth, and is delivered right to your e-mail account.

Speaking: Laddie Blaskowski has presented hundreds of speeches and programs to companies and professional organizations. He is available for keynote speeches and half-day or full-day training sessions. For more information on topics, visit our website at www.businesstruths.com/speaker.htm or call us at 719-260-7170.

Workshops: BusinessTruths® Consulting, Inc. offers workshops for business owners to help them with business growth issues in a group environment that fosters encouragement, interaction and insight from other entrepreneurs. Visit our website at www.businesstruths.com/workshops.htm for more information.

Additional Resources: We offer tools to help you discover new ways to succeed in your business. Visit our website at www.business truths.com/resources.htm to learn more.

Additional Contact Information: laddie@ businesstruths.com; judy@businesstruths.com; 719-260-7170

We want to hear from you!

If you have thoughts or comments about this book, or stories about how it has helped your business, we would love to hear from you. Please email us at: comments@business truths.com.

Acknowledgments

We would like to thank everyone who assisted with completing this book, from proofreading to reviewing our rough manuscript: Bruce Beebe, Mike Patterson, Sean Johnson, Michelle Smith, Karen Mitchell, Bill Smith, Shar Raat, Kristen Knoeckel, Mike Quaite, Marilyn Ross, Sue Collier, Dave Thomason, and Karsten and Rebecca Musaeus. We thank you all for taking time out of your busy schedules to help us with this project. Your comments, suggestions and prayers have been greatly appreciated!

We're especially grateful to Ken Blanchard, Noreen King, Winslow "Bud" Johnson, Kraig W. Kramers, Ronald Chernak, and Dirk Hobbs for so graciously offering your valuable time to read and endorse this book.

Most of all, we thank God the Father and the Lord Jesus Christ for the talents and blessings you've given us—we couldn't have completed this project without you!

About the Authors

Laddie Blaskowski is the president of BusinessTruths® Consulting, Inc., a company he founded in 1989 to help business owners create companies that are not only financially successful but also allow them to achieve their personal goals. Having himself owned a number of companies, he understands the concerns business owners face on a daily basis, particularly relating to business growth. This experience, combined with his background in banking and bank consulting, gives Laddie unique insight into what makes businesses successful. Laddie believes that the entrepreneurial spirit and those who have it are the engines that drive the United States economy.

Laddie received his MBA from Northwestern University's Kellogg Graduate School of Management. He strongly believes in community service, and has served on a number of boards, including a term as board chair of his region's chapter of the American Red Cross. He has also served as an evaluator for the Better Business Bureau and is active in his church, where he teaches adult Sunday school.

Judy Blaskowski is a professional writer and president of Dimpledott Connections, Inc., a firm providing specialized writing services. She has personally ghostwritten more than 300 published business articles, numerous grants for non-profit organizations, articles for non-profit publications, and articles for various newspapers.

She works with Laddie in their consulting firm, BusinessTruths® Consulting, Inc., and in their other business enterprises as operations director and publications director. Judy is a certified paralegal and holds a real estate specialty certification. She has been a member of various community boards and committees, and serves on the worship team at her church.

Laddie and Judy live in Colorado and are the proud parents of adult sons, Sean and Patrick, and the devoted owners of two extremely spoiled dogs.

Give the Gift of
The Step Dynamic™
to Your Friends and Colleagues

CHECK YOUR LEADING BOOKSTORE
OR ORDER HERE

❒ **YES**, I want _____ copies of *The Step Dynamic*™ at
$19.95 each, plus $4.95 shipping per book (Colorado
residents please add $1.48 sales tax per book).
Canadian orders must be accompanied by a postal
money order in U.S. funds. Allow 15 days for delivery.

❒ **YES**, I am interested in having Laddie Blaskowski
speak or give a seminar to my company, association,
or organization.

My check or money order for
$_____ is enclosed.

Please charge my: ❒ Visa ❒ MasterCard

❒ Discover ❒ American Express

Card # _____

Exp. Date _____ Signature _____

Name _____

Organization _____

Address _____

City/State/Zip _____

Phone _____

E-mail _____

Please make your check payable and return to:
Business Truths Consulting, Inc.
6660 Delmonico Dr.; Suite D-296
Colorado Springs, CO 80919

To order, visit www.BusinessTruths.com

Or call your credit card order to: 719-260-7170,
fax to: 719-531-5409
Call for bulk pricing.